How To Promote Events And Growth Your Team Step By Step From Newbies To Professional

Introduction

Businesses all over the world have used traditional methods of promotion and advertisement for years. These have included exposure in television and newspapers, as well as spreading the word through word of mouth and through the use of flyers. However, these methods do not really work in general because they do not target a specific audience, and people are usually tired of these methods of advertisement.

However, a new way of promoting products, one that will help consumers actually experience the products for themselves, has become popular recently. This new technique, called event planning, has been used by companies to encourage new customers to try their products and services for themselves for free before they buy it.

In addition to trying things out for free, companies have also used this strategy in networking in order to impart experiences and information to guests, while at the same time encouraging them to join in the business.

For any new business, event marketing is the best strategy to choose if getting new customers interested is what they are aiming for.

If you are thinking of using this technique in order to get people talking about your business, there are some things you should know first before you do anything. Event marketing is a complex process — it not only involves a lot of preparation and hard work, but also requires your full commitment as a businessperson.

Here, in this book, you will be provided with everything you need to know about starting your own networking event, as well as tips on how you can empower and reach out to both newbies and professionals through the events that you are going to establish. In the end, the investment you have put in event marketing usually pays off very well, with customers extremely satisfied and looking for more. Isn't that what every business is aiming for?

Thanks for downloading this book. I hope you enjoy it!

Chapter One: What Is Event Marketing?

Today, there are so many different ways of endorsing new products and services to potential customers. Gone are the days when companies simply relied on the use of television commercials or newspaper ads in order to get people interested in their product or service. Now, businesses can get in touch with their customers and actually let them experience the product for themselves as a way to encourage them to buy it.

This new technique in advertising is what experts call event marketing. Event marketing is a strategy used to promote a specific brand that involves face-to-face interaction between the business and its targeted customers. This usually happens in major social events such as concerts, sporting events, or fairs. Oftentimes, companies would make use of entertainment such as parties, contests, or shows in order to get the attention of consumers, who would then be enticed into sampling the products.

This is an effective strategy because people voluntarily agree to try out the product out of the mere fact that they were entertained or enthused by the business's presentation. When the attention of the customers is caught, it would provide the business with the opportunity to sell.

The value that comes with event marketing is way higher than what can be achieved through traditional methods like word of mouth or online ads. Charity alignments, discounts, free samples, or fun events are things which make the customers feel like they are being provided benefits in real life — as opposed to simply watching a commercial or reading a print advertisement.

Event marketing, especially when it comes to networking events, receive their success because they are different from the mainstream method of advertising. The impression that event marketing makes on customers lasts longer than what traditional methods can give, because these events provide meaningful and useful experiences to the consumers.

Chapter Two: Things You Should Remember When Planning An Event

In the United States alone, event marketing is a big industry, with investments from different companies reaching $300 billion on an annual basis. Conceived events can include tradeshows, webinars, golf hospitality functions, product launches, and customer conferences.

Event marketing is a unique business because each networking event or business conference is different from one another. Companies have aims of their own, and it is not always similar to the objectives of other companies. Therefore, marketing teams who are planning an event necessarily do not need, nor would they be able to find, a universal plan which would apply to all types of event marketing campaigns.

Instead of looking for a general instruction, you and your marketing team must plan your event on a tactic that is based on your own brand, which will be coupled by the nature of the event you want to create. Approaching each event by thinking that they are unique will provide you with the opportunity to make the best impact out of your own event.

When developing a marketing plan, there are aspects which you and your marketing team must consider.

- Personality. What personality is your brand trying to show to the audience? There have been brands in the past who have sought to make themselves look like peace bringers. There are also other brands which have tried being a friendly companion. There are also products that promote the simple joys of life.

  Take Coca-Cola as an example. Coca-Cola has always placed their soft drink product as a bringer of happiness and global peace. In this regard, the company dispensed their products in vending machines scattered across the globe, making it seem like they are making happiness available to anyone, anywhere.

- Target audience. The second thing that a company must always remember when establishing a marketing event is the audience to whom it should be catering.

  There has been an event popularized by men's health advocates called "Movember," which is a month-long moustache growing competition in November. The event was launched as a way to raise prostate cancer awareness. You might be thinking that moustaches and cancer are totally unrelated subjects, and you would be right to think that. The event was created for younger men, which is the target audience that would most likely benefit from cancer awareness.

- Lasting impression. What mark would your event leave on the audience once it is done? What morals, or what messages or opinions about the business would they be leaving with after the event is finished?

There have been companies in the past which have shown how great their products were by testing it out in public. In 2006, Sony introduced a campaign wherein they launched 250,000 bouncing balls on the San Francisco streets. This was done to promote the color display of their new television.

Not only was the event memorable because of the fact that it introduced thousands of bouncing balls to the streets, but it was also memorable because it made an impact by giving people an idea about what Sony's new televisions were actually capable of delivering.

Your event can also opt to be more subtle instead of being bold and extravagant. There are companies who also make use of QR codes on branding materials and posters, which integrate virtual and physical branding in one. These QR codes will lead customers to the company's website, where they will be treated with special offers and discounts on the physical products.

There are also companies that make use of social media in order to increase their popularity. Many companies that are geared towards a younger audience make use of social media websites such as Facebook and Twitter to raise their popularity. These companies provide freebies or discounts to their customers if they simply "like" the company Facebook page, if they follow the company on Twitter, or if they post a picture of themselves with the product on Instagram.

Chapter Three: Questions To Ask Yourself

Of course, just like with any other endeavor, in order to make a successful event marketing campaign, you should have a goal in mind, and you should have a plan laid out in order to reach that goal. Many event marketing strategies have failed in the past because of poor management, and because they were focused on all the wrong things.

Business owners often ask doubting questions which can usually only be answered if they try event marketing. These include:

- Networking events and business conferences take a huge amount of time to prepare and to maintain. They would take a lot of your energy from actually maintaining the business to endorsing it instead. Would the benefits that you get from your efforts in event marketing be worth it?

- Building relationships while expanding your network can be a tough task, so is it really feasible? If you step into the shoes of your consumer and you attend a networking event, would you actually get a good return of investment from it?

- Would it be possible to make yourself successful in all areas of your life just by planning and executing your networking events right?

The answer to these questions is a big YES!

What you need to do is to carefully plan your activity first before you get yourself into any actual execution. Regardless of where you are and from where your business stands, you can be successful just by following the simple rules and by using the tools provided here.

These event marketing campaigns can also provide an opportunity for you to improve the professional conditions of your co-workers. You can use the opportunity provided for you in making this event in order to empower and inspire newbies into becoming effective and efficient professionals in the networking world.

Before you are able to actually start planning your activity, you need to ask first a couple of questions to yourself. These include:

- How do you reach your intended audience? You are going to be hosting an event which would not only endorse networking as a great way to make money and to make business, but you are also going to be encouraging individuals to make a change. How are you going to hit those targets? What would be your plan to reach that specific goal of being able to make an impact to your intended customer demographic?

- Is there a need to make use of celebrities in your presentation? Is your networking event new, or is it not receiving enough attention? If so, will it actually help if you get celebrities to come to your event to advertise the product for you? Mostly, this works, because celebrities have the power to sway the opinion of a large audience by simply using their looks, charisma, and their relationship with the product.

- What should I do in order to plan a press and analysis program in my event? Would there be any need for you to consult with someone outside your business before you create a plan, or would it be possible for you to make your own with just the people you work with?

Once you have managed to figure out the answers to these questions, you can begin preparing for your event.

Chapter Four: Marketing Your Networking Event

Networking events are naturally successful in their own accord. However, there are instances when endorsing these events to the public seem to be too difficult to accomplish. If you are unsure about how you could possibly endorse your event to the public, here are the steps you can follow to make sure your event does not flop and turns out to a big hit.

Generally speaking, networking events tend to be more formal than other forms of events. There is also much more effort put into naming and describing the event than in most of the other events, which can be successful just by putting the word "free" in their titles.

- Choose the right name for your event. The name of the networking event should be unique and enticing. Do not give your event an extremely generic title such as "small business seminar" or "networking event." Give it a twist, and make sure that people would notice — and remember — it right away.

- Provide a description of what the event is about. Many event organizers are not familiar with how to describe their own events. To make it simpler, describe your event to the attendees using this formula: Explain what the event is, who will attend, and why they *have* to attend. Provide the answers to these questions in as little as 100 words.

- Make the date easily accessible to guests. Your target audience can be pretty busy in their own accord, which means that there is a tendency for them to forget the event. To prevent this from happening, use an invitation feature which allows users to link the schedule of the event to their own plans. This makes it possible for your audience to save the date of your event.

- Provide directions for your attendees. People would not be so keen in attending your events if they do not know how to get to where it is going to take place. You may be conducting your business in an old property, a mall, or in a company building, but regardless of where it happens, you should link the invites of your guests to apps such as Google Maps or Waze to make it easier for them to get to your event venue.

- Provide online registration for your guests. Of course, it would be necessary to have your guests register for the event. To make it simpler, you can provide them with a website where they can register.

- You might also want to promote your event not just through mailing lists, but through the Internet in general. If this is your plan, you would need to provide a website for your company or for your event. Building an online presence will help make your events more popular and successful. To make a website that will catch the attention of your target audience, here are some tips you can keep in mind.

- Be consistent in your branding. When you are consistent with how you brand your product, you will add legitimacy to the events you are planning, and it will make you look more professional in the eyes of your audience. It helps if your website's homepage looks like an event invitation, since it would look more professional and appealing that way.

- Provide your audience with direct contact. Aside from linking your invitations to the calendars of your recipients, as well as to Google Maps and/or Waze for the directions, you can also provide your email address as a way for people to have a direct contact to someone who has direct involvement in the event itself. This way, you would be able to respond to the questions that your attendees may have.

- Expound more on what the event is about. Your event homepage provides a great amount of customizability, which means that it will provide you with a great opportunity to give more information about the event.

Aside from these, you should also improve your online registration forms. Of course, your website will also serve as an online registration form to your attendees. This is something which you should put considerable focus on since it will provide you and your marketing team with a lot more information about your key demographic or your target audience. To make the registration process more helpful for you as a business, here are some improvements that you can make.

- Collect your attendees' personal and business information. This will help you keep track of what businesses are being represented in various networking events. To do this, ask your guests to provide you with business cards, email addresses, and other relevant information.

- Give your guests the option of informing others of what they are attending. This gives a new element to the registration, and definitely helps in spreading word about your business. In its essence, networking is all about building bridges and making connections with people. If guests are given the opportunity to see the names of people who are going to be attending the event, they will be able to determine how many opportunities the event will provide them.

- Give your guests the option of joining your mailing list. In the registration form, provide a box which your guests can imply check if they wish to sign up for email newsletters, instead of just signing them up automatically. Here, you can emphasize that they can get more information about new and upcoming networking events if they sign up go the email list.

Never add any person to your email list without asking their permission first. This is a very easy way for your emails to be marked as spam, so instead of forcing people into your email list and sending them newsletters even if they do not want to receive them, have them volunteer for it instead so that only the ones that are interested would be notified of upcoming events.

Chapter Five: Making Your Event Popular And Recurring

Networking events do not necessarily need to be one-off events. They can happen multiple times within a year, even if you only have one topic to discuss. This happens because people continue to be intrigued and interested with the topic of your event, which makes them come back for more.

Getting the attention of both newbies and professionals is tough at first. However, you can increase the attendance of both these demographics in your next event by making sure that the next event that you are going to plan will be better than the last one that you have done.

<u>Collecting Information From the Last Event</u>

Gather feedback from your most recent event. Unless you have already experienced running a networking event before, chances are you do not have any idea yet of how you are going to market the next one. So, ask people what they think of the networking event that had just finished. This will provide you with an important resource, which is the opinion of the attendees. This will provide you with information about what worked in your event, and which aspects need to be improved. Ask them the following questions:

- Did they like the event as a whole?
- What made them interested in taking part in the event?

- Would they encourage others to attend similar events?

- What do they think could you have done better in the event?

Aside from these, identifying the demographic of your guests, which you can do with the use of the registration forms, can also help you determine which parts of society are most interested in your event.

With your marketing team, create a unifying theme for your series of networking events. Regardless if you are going to invite a new speaker for every event, or if you are going to be holding a mixer, you need a consistent approach and style to your event. This will make running your event much easier, and it will help your guests set expectations.

Test your ideas in your next event. Even if you are simply sending emails to a few names to identify if they would be interested in taking part in your event, it would greatly help you if you would get that information just to make sure that you are on the right track.

Planning Your Next Event

After you have thought of a theme you can use for your next events, the next thing to do is to actually start planning the first one in the series. Planning more than one event at the same time is also a good idea, given that you will give yourself a chance to make slight changes to the events as they draw closer to the actual date. This will allow you to perform similar tasks together, such as choosing the location of your events.

Make a marketing plan for your event. This must be done individually, and not as a whole for the entire series. Even though this requires more effort, it is an important aspect in order for you to get more people to attend your events.

Make An Online Presence

Simply follow the steps indicated in the previous chapter. Create a website for your event, and make sure that you get as much information about your guests as possible for future reference.

Creating a website should be done one event at a time. Do not make a website for the whole string of events that you have planned. The best thing to do is: Once you are finished creating one website for the next event, start planning your website for the next one.

Promoting the Series as a Whole

Aside from just making an online presence and including people on email lists, there are a lot of other ways which you can use in order to get people talking about your upcoming networking events. One practical promotional method is using relevant event calendars. Others include group newsletters, local newspapers, and online forums.

You would want your events to be known to as many people as possible, and that is why it is important to have varying methods of promotion to use. You can also ask the help of social media users and popular bloggers to spread the word about your event. With everyone being so obsessed with being online all the time, there is a big chance that they will take notice of your advertisement in social media sites.

Bloggers also have a deeper relationship with their publishers and their followers, making them a much more reliable method of spreading the news about your networking events. They can influence their publishers to publish your advertisements in other forms of mass media such as newspapers, which in turn will give your networking events a better chance of getting the attention of more and more people.

You should also constantly push out updates to your event followers on social networking sites and other platforms. Even though promotion of a series may not be your highest priority, given that you may also need to sell the product or service yourself, you should still allot a part of your time in providing updates to your guests.

Always Plan Your Next Event

Never stop planning. Never stop being excited about what is to come in the future. One of the worst things that can possibly happen in networking events is when the organizers themselves become bored of what they are doing. This is not even uncommon, and they would usually just organize three or four events before they get distracted with other things.

Getting the attention of your target audience, both newbies and seasoned professionals, requires your one hundred percent. Regardless if you are doing it for your own or for someone else's benefit, you have to make sure that you are always looking forward to the next event. Building more momentum will make it easier for you to keep your business forging ahead.

In addition, if you constantly make improvements in your networking event series, there is a huge chance that someone will take notice of your efforts and actually offer you help. Whether or not you want these new people to help you out is totally up to you, but if you do not put your focus on your events, you might not even get this chance anyway.

It is important for you to think of your networking events as an extension of your business opportunities, and as a valuable way to make your business more successful. If event marketing was such a flop, no one would even bother doing it. But if you noticed, many companies are willing to spend money on it because it works well for them. Event marketing helps your business in enticing more people to make business with you, and it also provides your customers with a unique opportunity to experience your products and services.

Conclusion

In order for you to empower people and encourage them to participate in your networking events, make sure that you know what they want and that you would be able to deliver quality output for your future customers. Through this, not only will your event be successful, but your guests will leave with something that they have learned through what you have tackled in the event. Everybody goes home happy, and your business will gain more attention.

The next step for you now is to start planning your networking event, keeping in mind all the tips that have been shared to you in this book. Use that knowledge well, and good luck!

Series of this book

How To Build Network Marketing Leader Step By Step From Newbies To Professional

http://www.amazon.com/gp/product/B019LP3UU6/ref=s9_simh_gw_g351_i2_r?ie=UTF8&fpl=fresh&pf_rd_m=ATVPDKIKX0DER&pf_rd_s=desktop-1&pf_rd_r=0P0B8QD7SA97MPRYB56Y&pf_rd_t=36701&pf_rd_p=2079475242&pf_rd_i=desktop

www.ingramcontent.com/pod-product-compliance
Lightning Source LLC
Chambersburg PA
CBHW070310190526
45169CB00004B/1573